Woodstock
Vision

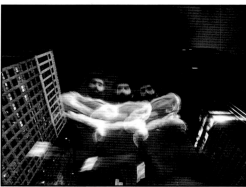

SELF-PORTRAIT '78

Elliott Landy

Woodstock Vision

The Spirit of a Generation

With an Afterword
by Richie Havens

CONTINUUM — NEW YORK

To Joiwind and Bo for being my children and bringing me such Joy,
my mother and sisters for their love and support,
and to Diana, my partner in life, with Love.

1994
The Continuum Publishing Company
370 Lexington Avenue, New York, NY 10017

Printed in Italy

Library of Congress Cataloging-in-Publication Data

Landy, Elliott
    Woodstock Vision, The Spirit of a Generation / text and photos by Elliott Landy
        p.   cm.

    ISBN 0-8264-0662-9 — ISBN 0-8264-0663-7 (pbk.)
    1. Photojournalism — United States. 2. Popular culture — United States. 3. Photojournalists — United States — Biography. 4. Landy, Elliott. 5. United States — Social life and customs — 1945-70. 6. Rock musicians — United States — Portraits. I. Title.
TR 820.L37 1994
770 .92—dc20
[B]
                                              94-1274
                                                CIP

Design Direction: **Elliott Landy**
Design: **Mark Hecker**
Cover: **Renee Samuels, Joiwind Landy**
Production Consultant: **Steve Baron**

Dedication

I love photography. It has always been good to me. It has taken me to the places I wanted to go, helped me meet some of the people I wanted to meet, and allowed me to share with others some of my deepest experiences.

I was lucky. In the early days of my career I chose to photograph people and events that later came to be socially and culturally significant. But when I was photographing Jim Morrison in the Hunter College Auditorium, or Janis Joplin in the Anderson Theater on New York's Lower East Side, neither event had, then or now, any meaning for me beyond my momentary love of the music they were creating and the way they looked creating it. The thrill, the inspiration of the moment was all there was. To capture a flickering moment of joyous experience and share it with others — that was the reason I began photographing in the first place, and that is still the reason I take pictures today. I was never a fan.

In between the beginning and now, the chance to earn a living at what I loved to do occurred and so I took it and kept taking it, and to this sort of chance in life, I dedicate this book.

Try to be happy, try to have fun, and try to share this happiness and fun with those around you, and may God (the universal experience) expand your conception of happiness to include helping those near you who need help. And may communication bring all of us on this planet closer together, closer to God, closer to each other.

Elliott Landy
Woodstock,
New York
August 1994

Photo: L. Landy

THE AUTHOR, 1970

5

The Vision of a Generation

There was a terrible war raging in Vietnam in the Sixties. We, the Woodstock Generation, knew it was wrong and fought against it. We didn't care what the social penalties were — we stood our ground and said, "No, this is wrong. I love my country and will not participate in this immoral action which destroys the principles our country was built on."

At the same time, music was reaching us. It got us so excited that we felt a deep part of ourselves which we had not been in touch with before. It was wild, and its wildness freed us from cultural restraints, from the uptightness that habits place on a human being. So people were free to be naked in public, to talk about having sex, to smoke grass openly with friends, take acid, have long hair, dress any way they chose, to experiment and explore life freely.

I was a young photographer looking for a way to publish my work. I was a human being, hurt and injured by the injustice of the war. I was a person who smoked grass occasionally and loved to listen to music. When I was stoned, I always wanted to take pictures. I combined all these elements into an attempt to make my life good. I wanted to earn money, make beautiful pictures, listen to music, and help the world.

Everything seemed to be changing. Established ideas and institutions, in every sphere, were being challenged. It seemed like the world was about to change profoundly because people would not be able to go on living the way they had been. It was a time of hope.

The frontiers of consciousness were being expanded. We were exposed to Eastern philosophy, metaphysical books, psychedelics, rock music, and grass.

Rock concerts were rites of passage, where people came to be together, to see the bands, and to get high from the music, the dance, and the drugs. The goal was to transcend the mundane vision of everyday life by reaching an ecstatic state. We were unknowingly using methods similar to those found in the traditions of indigenous peoples throughout history.

Pop music had not yet become an international business and cultural phenomenon. Rock 'n' roll was outside the norm of society, part of the "underground" culture, and to be involved with it made you an outsider. A new group of people who believed in alternatives to the American Way of Life was galvanized by this new, free form of raucous music. A world of hippies, drugs, free love, metaphysics, and political activism was born.

The musicians themselves could as easily have been members of the audience as performers onstage, and often they did mingle with the crowds after the show. There was a true feeling of solidarity, a unity of purpose, and the purpose was to change the world. *We want the world, and we want it NOW!* was the anthem sung by Jim Morrison. We thought that the freedom to behave as we wished, coupled with the power of music to liberate the soul, would emancipate the world.

The Sixties were about trying to discover the truth about everything and trying to live that truth in life. Discovering your inner self, and being true to it. Doing what you really wanted to do, and trusting that if you did the right thing, "your way" would be in alignment with The Way, (as in the ancient Chinese text *The Way of Life*) and the universe would support you by making the right things happen for you. People tried to earn the money they needed from "work" they loved.

The Sixties were also about looking for happiness and trying to create perfection and justice for everyone on the planet. For the first time a mass culture saw itself as totally interconnected to all other beings and began to take on a global rather than a local responsibility. The tools we used were love, freedom, spirituality, music, and action. We demanded freedoms long held to be taboo—to have sex at will, to use consciousness-expanding substances—and we actively tried to change the establishment through righteous, inspired action.

A lot of other things changed as well. Before the Sixties, men had short hair and crew cuts and wore business suits and ties. Social conformity prevented them from wearing frilly shirts and earrings. But the Sixties emancipated men's creative and feminine side. Freedom

THE WHO, ANDERSON THEATER, 1968

replaced formality. Men not only let their hair and beards grow and put on more colorful clothes, they also smiled more lovingly and became more accepting of others. So many people were naked that men began to accept real women's bodies instead of focusing on *Playboy* fantasies. They concentrated more on feelings and emotions than on physical satisfaction—something only women had done before. Women and men became better friends. Instead of guys just hanging out together, talking dirty, and harassing women, a new situation arose: men and women hung out together, smoked dope, had sex, and listened to rock 'n' roll. A communal experience was born. Men began cooking and taking care of children, while women got into rock 'n' roll.

Thus the education and upbringing of chil-

dren began to change. Children were carried around with their parents, brought to parties, and learned to sleep in a car. Home was any place where the road stopped. Children no longer stayed home with baby-sitters; parents started, more and more, to bring their kids with them, and the kids were much better off.

Drugs were a part of that interconnectedness, but they were light, nonaddicting, consciousness-raising natural herbs, which helped us attain higher states. Unlike hyperaggressive drugs, such as cocaine, they made us more mellow, more loving, more sensitive, and more open.

Grass was special — you shared it. We had been taught to keep our possessions to ourselves, but when you smoked grass, you offered it to whoever happened to be nearby, whether you were in the street or at a rock concert. Being "high" opened people up to themselves and to others. Smoking was a communal activity and often created an instant bonding, even if it sometimes lasted only a short time.

Since you were more mellow when you were "high," you were able to listen and to perceive more. You could really 'get into another person's trip,' sit and play with a baby for hours, or "see" a flower for what seemed like the first time. In some ways drugs worked similarly to meditation, reducing the perceptual blocks and illusions of separateness we learned from our Western cultural upbringing.

One of the main visions which permeated the Sixties culture was of the brotherhood of man. Many people were initially able to perceive this truth because of grass and other consciousness-enhancing drugs.

The Woodstock Generation rediscovered many ancient spiritual truths and gave the contemporary world an alternative vision for living —to be loving, gentle, and open all the time. Drugs were a window to that vision, but there was a price to pay. When drugs are used to reach the highs, one is less capable of dealing graciously with the lows and responds negatively to situations that could be handled better. Reactions such as anger, depression, physical depletion, and dependency are common. The ultimate goal is to be able to experience and enjoy life: the freedom and the ecstasy of being in a loving state of mind, and the strength to experience the difficulties without being upset, uptight, or anxious.

Now we realize that we must reach that state, not through harmful chemicals, but through meditation and inner spiritual commitment to joy

SWAMI SATCHTANANDA, WOODSTOCK FESTIVAL

and love, coupled with the hard work of getting through life while maintaining our integrity.

We hoped to leave the existing society behind and do our own thing—find our own truths and way of life. The Sixties culture called for a rejection of material and traditional comforts. We no longer needed beds to sleep in. The floor and a mat would do. Insurance plans, new cars, new clothes, traditional ceremonies, nine-to-five jobs, meaningless work done just to pay the bills—all were questioned and discarded.

What was important was to get high, to feel yourself, to become one with the spiritual forces in the universe, to communicate with our fellow man. So what if we lived in houses that would never be ours, drove cars that were falling

apart, wore clothes that were used when we got them? As long as we shared what we had with each other, we would be all right. We felt we could live a nomadic, transient life as long as we were loving and generous.

We also thought meaningless middle-class values would disappear. Little did we realize then that in every historical phase there is a dialectic in which first one, then an opposite action predominates, followed by a synthesis of the two.

The yuppies of the Eighties, with their total focus on material wealth and meaningless status symbols, were a reaction to the drop-out, turn-on, tune-in hippie culture of the Sixties.

The energy created during that time is still with us, slowly influencing us more and more. It has evolved into what is today called New Age thought. The inheritors of "Woodstock" are not only the tie-dyed young people we see at concerts, but also the healers, the spiritual practitioners, and the activists who support the diversity of planetary life-forms. Many young people are intuitively drawn to the Woodstock era, feeling a closeness they don't yet fully understand while taking inspiration from its lifestyles.

Perhaps the Nineties will be a time of synthesis for the two ways of thinking and being, for balancing a spiritual awareness of our place in the universe with an ability to work toward making physical life on this planet more pleasant for everyone. What we of the Sixties generation have learned is that the material part of life is important as well. As the I Ching says, the ultimate manifestation of Heaven is on Earth.

Stars and Stones

In 1967 a lot of things were wrong with America and I felt I had to say something about what was going on. I wanted to take pictures that explained the truth to people and presented them with alternatives. I worked with several underground newspapers, and chose what I wanted to photograph. A police press pass gave me special access to events.

At peace demonstrations I saw a lot of violence and police brutality. The police almost always provoked the violence, an aspect of the situation the mainstream press was not reporting. Newspaper accounts of demonstrations I had been to bore little relation to the experience I had had, almost as if the reporters had been to a different demonstration.

The establishment media devoted more space to movie stars, corporate announcements, and singular violent crimes than to an expression of social and human conscience by tens of thousands of people.

One night there was a demonstration against South African diamond mines, on Fifth Avenue near Rockefeller Center. The police charged into the peaceful picket line and began hitting people with nightsticks. Everyone ran, but the police caught up with one young man who had a limp and beat him to the ground for no reason whatsoever. I took a picture.

ROBERT KENNEDY, ROCKEFELLER CENTER, 1968

Someone yelled that Bobby Kennedy was right below us in the ice-skating rink.

I ran down and told him that the police were beating people on the street above, naively expecting him to immediately run upstairs and stop it. He was cautious, obviously not wanting or able to get personally involved. I was surprised by his reluctance to get involved. He sent an aide to see what was happening. By that time it was over.

I then rushed my film to the Associated Press, one of the largest press agencies in the world. After the film was processed, the editors saw the picture and told me, "No, it's not for us, we don't want it." That was the first time I had any personal contact with those involved with the news that the world reads, and I saw that they were closed to the truth. It was just as shocking to me as the police brutality I had photographed. The people who controlled the media disliked hippies and were against the demonstrations. Their failure to report events truthfully was not an oversight.

So the pictures were published in the underground press, whose editors sometimes went too far the other way, dehumanizing and condemning anyone who was not on their side — urging anger and aggression rather than peaceful resolution of conflict.

That police brutality was not an isolated incident. I saw it often at other demonstrations. After a while I found the dynamic of many peace demonstrations to be a game between the police and the demonstrators. The question was not who was right or wrong but whether or not you wanted to play that game. You could be the policeman or the demonstrator, but either way you were still part of the fighting. The "isness" of the situation was conflict.

During this time I also took photographs at celebrity press parties because I wanted to be part of the glamorous world which I had seen in media all my life. The famous and would-be-famous went to be seen, publicized, glamorized, and admired. No one was really having fun. It

A SMILE ON OPENING NIGHT, NYC, 1968

was an ego trip. They painted themselves and made believe they were beautiful, saying in effect, "My breasts are beautiful, my eyebrows are beautiful," but no one said, "My mind is beautiful, my heart is beautiful." It was too artificial for me, and I never felt good about being there. I saw that Hollywood celebrities had no real relationship to my life.

At one awards ceremony Dustin Hoffman told me how ridiculous he thought these events were, and he was obviously uncomfortable about having to be there. We were in a room with chintzy flowered wallpaper, rows of chairs with the actors' names pasted on them, and the actors were lined up like cattle going to slaughter. The absurdity of the star culture with its hero worship, prize awards, and contrived media coverage

seemed obvious to us both.

It struck me that when you watch a film or a television show, what you see goes inside your head and registers as truth, as reality. This impression goes beyond what you think about it, and becomes part of you, almost like a stamp on your brain. It seemed sad that the whole world was so obsessed with these people because of the illusions created by the films they were in. It was all make-believe, and the truth became visible through my lens.

The photographs that came from these events were often ridiculous, to the point of being humorous. I never meant to take a "bizarre" picture of anyone: they happened by chance and showed me more about what was going on at those parties than I realized while I was there. The camera saw more than I did. It penetrated the illusion of glamour.

I also realized that photographs say just as much about the photographer as they do about the subject. The photos of the press parties exude such an unpleasant atmosphere because I felt out of place at these events. Other photographers, standing next to me, produced traditional, glamorous movie-star images. My pictures reflected that aspect of the events which impacted most on me—the falseness and superficiality. They were a reflection of my inner feelings toward what was happening—a flow of energy, channeled and filtered through my own person. My camera never lied, and taught me much about what I was seeing.

During that time I also discovered the

grace of chance. By letting myself be carried along by circumstances at the press parties or peace demonstrations, I would accidentally get perfectly composed images—images that were more interesting to me than if I had been able to shoot one which was visually composed in a traditional way.

Many of my best photographs were made because I had no desire to push aside the people who were standing in front of me. I just held my camera above my head and let myself go with the crowd. From those experiences I learned that chance is one of the most important and useful things in life. I would advise anyone who is serious about photography to try taking pictures without looking through the viewfinder.

With this negative atmosphere prevailing at most peace demonstrations and press parties, I lost interest in photographing them. I had done it. The situations were repetitive, and the pictures began to sour. I wasn't interested in showing violence or people looking strange. I was interested in beauty. I discovered I was an artist, not a violent revolutionary.

PEARL BAILEY, MORT GLANKOFF, CUE MAGAZINE AWARDS DINNER

PHOTOS ON PAGES 11 TO 20 WERE TAKEN IN 1967 OR 1968 IN NEW YORK CITY UNLESS OTHERWISE NOTED.

LAUREN
BACALL,
FILM
AWARDS
CEREMONY

DEMONSTRATION AGAINST SOUTH AFRICAN DIAMOND MINING

PENTAGON PEACE DEMONSTRATION, WASHINGTON, D.C.

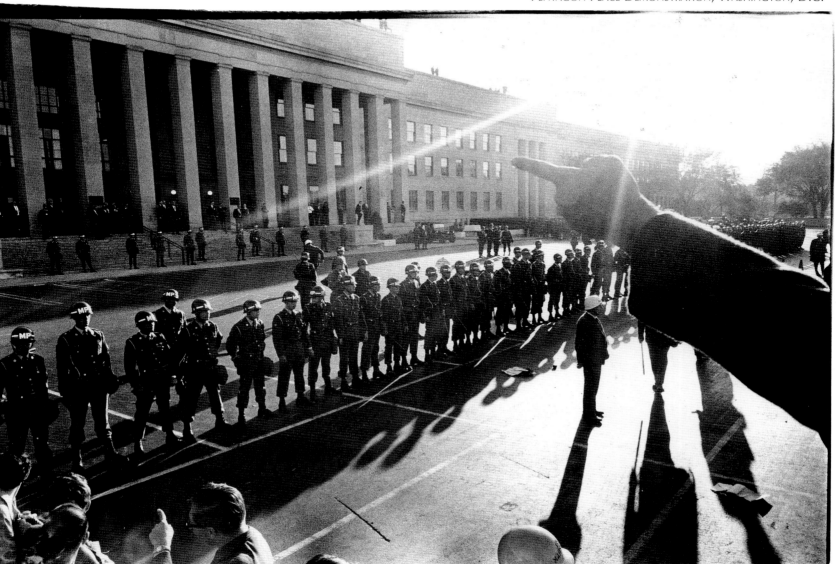

PENTAGON PEACE DEMONSTRATION, WASHINGTON, DC, 1967

DEMONSTRATION
AGAINST SOUTH
AFRICAN
DIAMOND
MINING

HOLLYWOOD PRODUCER DARRYL F. ZANUCK

MARLENE DIETRICH, HIDING FROM PHOTOGRAPHERS' FLASHBULBS AT PARTY AFTER PREMIERE OF HER ONE-WOMAN BROADWAY SHOW

Hermione Gingold

Peace Demonstration, Times Square

Policeman hitting Demonstrator w. Blackjack, Wash. Sq. Park

Too Late for the Red Carpet

PENTAGON PEACE DEMONSTRATION, WASHINGTON, D.C.

PRO WAR DEMONSTRATOR AT PENTAGON DEMONSTRATION

PEACE DEMONSTRATION

FAYE DUNAWAY

JOAN COLLINS

ABORTION RIGHTS DEMONSTRATION

High on the Music

The appeal of musicians of the Sixties was that they played from a very deep, very personal, very poetic part of themselves. They tried to express the essence of themselves through their music. Musicians had always tried to express this essence, of course. But in the Sixties they consciously looked for it and went beyond the norms of society to develop a new form of music created as a participatory experience for the audience. They did not simply perform, but interacted with the audience, inviting them to dance, to change their life-styles, to become part of a large family of like-minded beings. The concert space became a communal space for an evening.

If the Sixties generation wanted to change the world, the musicians were

PROCOL HAREM W. JOSHUA LIGHT SHOW, FILLMORE EAST, NYC, 1968

viewed as the leaders. We confused their art with their personalities. As artists they had discovered how to tap into the essence of the time, how to utilize masses of energy to move people and communicate their *feelings*. In so doing they created a powerful transformative experience for a culture in the midst of an evolutionary elevation of awareness.

But the musicians, so successful at their art, often didn't reach that same level in their personal lives—some failed abysmally—nor were they necessarily gurus in areas other than music. Dylan tried to make this clear to me when we met by denying that he was a political leader.

I was never into the personalities of the performers whom I was photographing. When I was shooting a concert, only the music and how the musicians looked as they were playing it mattered. If I didn't like the music, I couldn't take pictures.

Above all, I was into photography for the *image*. Meaning and content were secondary. This was true even though I wanted to say something with my photos. I felt that the only way to *really* say something—to create a feeling in the person seeing the photograph—was to present a work of art so well composed that its form touched something within the viewer, helping him or her to open up and understand. Without first opening, a person cannot learn, and so I was a stickler for creative control over my work—especially since, in the beginning, I was not getting paid beyond bare costs for film and paper used to make the prints.

In 1968 two former legitimate Jewish theaters in New York's East Village began presenting psychedelic rock concerts—the Anderson, and Bill Graham's Fillmore East. They were located around the corner from the offices of *The Rat*, the underground newspaper that I was photographing for. I remember my first concert. Anyone would.

It was a new world of fabulous sound, music-filled air, friends everywhere sharing joints, and an incredibly synchronized Joshua Light Show. I was very inspired. It changed my life. I had to take pictures.

The Fillmore East opened in NYC on March 8, 1968. Big Brother and the Holding Company, with Janis Joplin was the headline act. They had just signed with CBS Records. It was a memorable evening.

I had free run of the house because the management of the theater—Bill Graham and John Morris—knew I was working for the underground press. There were very few other photographers, since photographs of rock music were not yet commercially viable. I was able to take pictures from wherever I chose, for as long as I wished, without being worried that an aggressive guard would come along and rip the cameras out of my hands, as began to happen in later years. There was no paranoia, and few restrictions. Today photographers are usually restricted to shooting the first three songs of a concert and are confined to the photographer's pit, directly in front of the stage — which is often not the best place to get a beautiful photograph.

Janis Joplin was one of the few performers I got to know personally while I was photographing in New York City. I

got an assignment from *New York* magazine, to go with Janis and Big Brother to Detroit, where they had a gig at the Grande Ballroom. There we were hosted by John Sinclair and MC-5, the reigning Detroit psychedelic band. Rock bands like Big Brother were part of an underground community which stretched across the nation. We hung out at MC-5's downtown communal apartment, which was big and rambling, with people smoking dope in every room.

In the MC5 commune, Detroit, 1968

I found Janis to be loving, considerate, and lonely. She seemed to experience pain even when she was having pleasure. That she couldn't get as high in real life as she did from her performances saddened and depressed her. Drugs got out of hand. They made the highs higher and the lows lower—too low. Her answer was to do more. She was wrong.

One night, after a big show in New York, I shared a cab with her and a few other members of the band. She directed the cab to drive to the home of a casual friend who she hoped was there. When she got out, she shook her head and with a sad smile said, "Man, what a drag. Here I am a big star and I can't find anyone to be with." We all invited her to stay with us, but she walked away. It was snowing. The cab drove on, taking each of us to our destinations, but for Janis, apparently, there was no place to call home.

PHOTOS ON PAGES 22 TO 63 WERE TAKEN IN 1967 & 1968 IN NEW YORK CITY UNLESS OTHERWISE NOTED.

THE WHO,
ANDERSON
THEATER

GRACE
SLICK,
FILLMORE
EAST

THE BEATLES,
PRESS
CONFERENCE,
NYC

THE FUGS, ANDERSON THEATER

SLY & THE FAMILY STONE, FILLMORE EAST

JEFFERSON AIRPLANE, FILLMORE EAST

MELANIE, WHERE SHE GREW UP, THE BRONX

RICHIE HAVENS

ALBERT KING, FILLMORE EAST

JOHN LEE HOOKER

CHUCK BERRY, FILLMORE EAST

FRANK ZAPPA, FILLMORE EAST

Taj Mahal, Newport Folk Festival

Joan Baez,
Newport Folk
Festival

PETE
SEEGER,
NEWPORT
FOLK
FESTIVAL

JOAN BAEZ & MIMI FARINA

RAMBLIN' JACK ELLIOTT

Joan Baez

Buddy Guy

Newport Folk Festival, 1968

Doc Watson

VAN AND JANET MORRISON, MOONDANCE ALBUM PHOTO SESSION, WOODSTOCK, 1970

ERIC CLAPTON,
DEREK & THE
DOMINOES,
1970

JIM MORRISON, HUNTER COLLEGE

JIM MORRISON, FILLMORE EAST

JIMI HENDRIX,
JOSHUA
LIGHT SHOW,
FILLMORE EAST

JIMI HENDRIX,
PRESS
CONFERENCE,
PAN AM
BUILDING

JIMI
HENDRIX,
FILLMORE
EAST

JIMI HENDRIX, PRESS CONFERENCE, JANUARY 1968

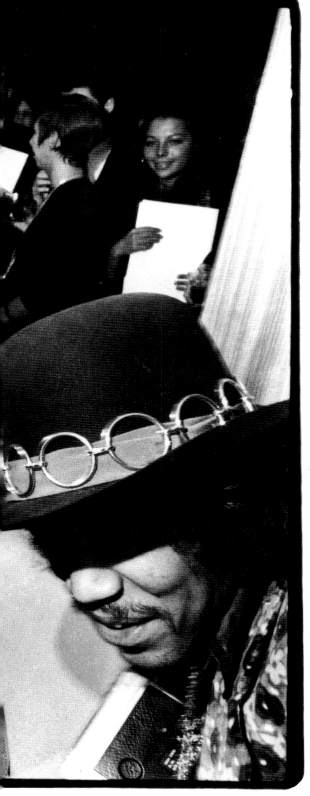

JIMI HENDRIX,
FILLMORE EAST

Janis Joplin

JANIS JOPLIN W. BIG BROTHER DRUMMER DAVE GETZ

JANIS JOPLIN,
NEWPORT
FOLK FESTIVAL, 1968

w. Andy Warhol and Tim Buckley at Max's Kansas City Restaurant

Ratner's Restaurant

Detroit Airport, 1968

NEWPORT FOLK FESTIVAL, 1968

ED SANDERS W. JANIS, ANDERSON THEATER

ALBERT GROSSMAN, BIG BROTHER & CLIVE DAVIS, PRES. CBS RECORDS.

W. ALBERT GROSSMAN

PRESS PARTY CELEBRATING CBS'S SIGNING OF BIG BROTHER AND THE HOLDING COMPANY

W. ALBERT GROSSMAN

W. CLIVE DAVIS

OPPOSITE PAGE:
TOP: OPENING NIGHT, FILLMORE EAST
BOTTOM: ANDERSON THEATER

LEANING ON ALBERT'S BACK

W. SAM ANDREW IN GROSSMAN'S OFFICE

GRANDE
BALLROOM,
DETROIT,
1968

W. BIG
BROTHER

The Band

One of the first major magazine assignments I got was to photograph Janis Joplin and Big Brother and the Holding Company. They were managed by Albert Grossman, who also managed Bob Dylan. Albert had a distinct dislike for me because of a run-in we had had at a Dylan concert a few months earlier, and he once asked me to leave his office in the middle of a shoot. However, he did allow me some access to his group because the job was for a major magazine.

One night, I was photographing Big Brother at a club called Generation, which later became Jimi

NEXT OF KIN

Hendrix's Electric Ladyland Studio. Albert was there, and in between sets, he motioned me into a tiny room in the back of the club. I didn't have a clue what was coming next. He then popped the question—was I "free to take some pictures this weekend in Toronto?" "Of who," I asked. "They don't have a name yet." I said yes.

At the time I didn't know how important that question was. It's funny how some moments stand out in your memory. I can still see the two of us in that tiny room. I had thought he was still mad at me.

Later Myra Friedman, Janis's friend and publicist, told me that Albert had seen the photos of Janis which I had left in her office, and he flipped over them. There was one in particular that showed her hugging him from behind at a press party. He was reaching around behind him while she cuddled up, looking like a little girl; she's kind of goofing a little bit, distracting him while he was doing business. Albert had "liberated" my print and put it on his wall.

It was admirable that Albert was able to forgive me once he recognized my talent. It was also smart. Intuitively he knew that I was the right photographer for the new album—"Music From Big Pink." He discovered me and gave me my big break. That night he also told me that Dylan might be there for the picture. I felt my life going into high gear.

The first time I heard The Band's music was the night I met Robbie Robertson and Garth Hudson to show them my photographs. After looking at my pictures in the hallway of the recording studio in New York, Robbie brought me into the mixing room where Garth was listening to his masterful organ intro to "Chest Fever" coming full blast from the finest studio speakers.

58

It was a good beginning. They asked me to meet them in Toronto the following week.

Three of the members of the group picked me up at the airport, and we drove up north to Rick Danko's uncle's farm to take the "next of kin" picture which appeared on the album. This was their way of acknowledging their families, and the importance of their roots to their music. Four of them were from Canada, and Levon Helm was from Arkansas. His parents couldn't make the trip, so we put their picture in the corner of the shot. Dylan didn't come either.

The guys in The Band were different from the other musicians I had been around. Even though they were young, hung out with the best of 'em, and did whatever "irresponsible" things they wanted, there was a deep wisdom and maturity about them. They

IN CANADA

knew about life and about people. You couldn't fool them. They had been around and had seen it all with a really deep comprehension. I liked all of them a lot and felt really comfortable around them—like a kindred soul.

I flew back to New York with John Simon, who had produced the album. When they saw the pictures from Toronto, they liked them, and we made plans to do a shot of the band members alone. On Easter weekend 1968 I went up to photograph them in Woodstock, where they were living in the house they jokingly called Big Pink. Four of them—Levon, Richard Manuel, Garth, and Rick—were living there. Robbie had his own house elsewhere in Woodstock, with his wife, Dominique, a French Canadian journalist.

It was in the basement of this house, that

they recorded the basement tapes with Dylan. All the instruments and microphones were set up. Dylan had originally rented the house for them when he brought them to Woodstock.

We took some pictures on Saturday, and I stayed overnight. The next day, Easter Sunday, they were invited to Bob's house, but couldn't bring me with them. I was left at Big Pink with Levon's girlfriend, who wasn't in the mood to go, she said.

We got stoned, and settled in. After a few hours she asked me to drive her somewhere. She wanted to find Levon. So we drove through winding wooded roads, up a mountain, and pulled off the road in front of a big old brown wooden house. As we were walking inside, she told me, "This is Bob's house."

Sara Dylan greeted us at the door, her inner warmth matching her physical beauty. She didn't know exactly who I was, but immediately made me feel welcome, offered me a drink, and invited me to be comfortable, which I definitely was not. In retrospect I think that her energy—who she was—was responsible for Bob's choosing a positive path at that point in his life.

I looked around the large living room: vaulted ceiling, dark wooden beams, picture window looking out over the trees, a big fireplace, and a grand piano in the corner. I saw a couple of the Band members there, and felt uneasy since they had not asked me to come.

After what now seems like less than a minute, Levon's girlfriend was back and wanted to leave. She hadn't found him and wanted to look further. So we left. I don't even know if I saw Bob or not. It was all too fast, but that was the first time I might have met him.

We drove down through some more winding Woodstock country roads and pulled up to another house. She knew the woman who lived there and suspected that Levon was 'visiting.' We parked the car, got out, and walked up to the house. There were several doors, and she went over to one on the other side, while I waited by the car. After a moment, Levon peeked out of another door, and asked me what was going on. I told him, and he told me to make believe I hadn't seen him. His girlfriend came back a minute later, having gotten no answer, and we left. I didn't say anything, and we drove back to Big Pink. It was quite a ride.

We took several beautiful photographs at Big Pink. One was a picture of them taken

OUTSIDE BIG PINK

from behind, sitting on a bench in front of a pond. They had explained that they didn't want a name because they wanted the focus to be on the music, not on themselves., and didn't want to be "labeled" and defined by the audience's preconceptions. They wanted to be free to change musically. So they wanted to stay almost anonymous, which I think we captured in that photograph.

But they didn't feel it was right, I don't know why. So I went back to do a second shoot. We did some nice shots at a few different places, but those weren't what they wanted either. But they decided to stick with me and try a third time. We had a real nice personal connection.

We talked about what was missing in the photos, and I showed them a book of pho-

tographs of the Old West and suggested we go for that look. They liked the idea.

I realized that the subjects of those photographs were very connected to the land, they seemed to be planted there. We looked around for the right place to take the shot and found it in their front yard.

The other element present in the old photographs was respect. People took the camera seriously. A photographer's visit was an important and unusual occasion. People stood up straight and looked right at the camera, which made them look dignified. People were a different sort in those days. They were connected to the earth, there were no modern conveniences. Of course, I couldn't have created that old-time classic look with just anyone. It was their spirits that came out and greeted the opportunity for self-expression.

I spent a lot of time in Woodstock, photographing, showing them the pictures, and just hanging out. They showed me the country life, and introduced me to their friends. I loved it. I went to Los Angeles to photograph them for their second album, *The Band*, which they were recording in Los Angeles, and for their debut performance at the Fillmore West in San Francisco.

They didn't ask me to do their third album, but by that time I wasn't interested in music photography anymore. I had done it and had a different creative direction plotted out.

Twenty-four years later, in 1993, I took photographs of Garth, Levon, Rick, and three other musicians when they made the first new Band album in fifteen years.

60

Big Pink

MUSIC FROM
BIG PINK,
ALBUM
PHOTO

LEVON HELM, FILLMORE EAST, NYC, 1969

ROBBIE & DOMINIQUE ROBERTSON, FILLMORE EAST, 1969

RICHARD MANUEL, AT HOME, 1968

BASEMENT OF RICK'S HOUSE, 1969

RECORDING THE BAND ALBUM, L.A., 1969

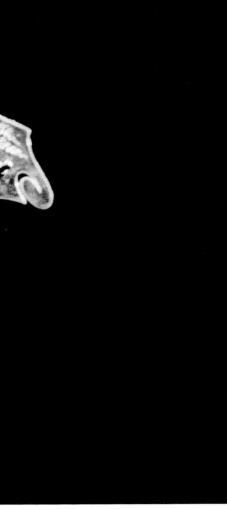

ROBBIE AND LEVON, UPSTAIRS AT RICK'S HOUSE, 1969

LEVON HELM, FILLMORE WEST, S.F., 1969

RICK DANKO W. HAMLET

PHOTOS ON FOLLOWING FOUR PAGES TAKEN FOR THE BAND ALBUM, WOODSTOCK, 1969

THE BAND, 1993

THE BAND, 1993
W. NEW MEMBERS

ABOVE: AT LEVON'S,
WOODSTOCK

LEFT: AT OPUS 40

GARTH HUDSON

RICK DANKO

Photographing Bob Dylan

The first time I photographed Dylan was at the Woody Guthrie Memorial Concert at Carnegie Hall in New York City in 1967. It was his first public appearance since his motorcycle accident a year earlier. He was playing with The Band, who were unknown at that time.

I was just starting my photographic career and wanted to see the show as well as take some pictures that I could sell. So I called up Dylan's office, identified myself as a photographer for an underground newspaper, and asked for two press tickets.

I brought my cameras to the concert, assuming that since they'd given me tickets as a photographer, I could take photographs. But when I got to Carnegie Hall, there were signs posted stating "No Photographs Allowed," and the ushers insisted that I check my cameras. I argued, showing my press pass and the tickets from Dylan's office, but to no avail. So I said, "OK, no pictures allowed," and checked half my cameras, but kept the other half—everything that would fit into my pockets and my date's bag.

I had a good seat near the front of the hall. Dylan came on stage, and I started snapping away, clicking my shutter only during the loud passages in order to be as discreet as possible.

After a couple of songs Arlene Cunningham, who worked for Dylan's manager, Albert Grossman, spotted me taking photographs. Soon she and Albert, whom I did not know at the

W. Rick Danko and Robbie Robertson at Guthrie concert

time, and a guard were all waving to me from the side of the hall telling me to stop taking photographs. I pretended not to see their increasingly frantic waving.

Then Albert gestured to the guard to get me out of the seat. Meanwhile Dylan was playing with The Band, and it was very exciting. The guard came toward me. I knew what was going to happen next. They always go for your film.

So I rewound the film I had shot and gave it to my lady friend, with instructions not to give it up under any circumstances. I quickly put another roll of film into the camera. I didn't want to create a scene and disrupt the concert, so we followed the guard out into the posh, carpeted, chandeliered lobby where Albert, Arlene, and a few other people quickly surrounded us.

Albert demanded the film, and I adamantly refused, acting as if it were gold. "There's *no* way I'm gonna give you *this* film." But Arlene had seen me switch and was trying to tell him, but he was too engrossed in the mock battle I was staging. Every time I heard Arlene say, "She's got the film!", I raised my voice a bit, repeating, "You're not gonna get *this* film! You have no right to do this," and so on. I really carried on—I wasn't violent or nasty, just loud, to distract him from her.

While I argued with him, I held the camera in front of me, presenting it to him without

78

being obvious about it, knowing he would grab it. Finally he did and ripped the film out, exposing it and making it even blanker, I guess. After that we left, with the film safely hidden away. It never bothered me that I missed the rest of the concert. Only the film mattered. That was the first time I saw Bob Dylan, and the last time I saw my lady friend.

Despite that first strange encounter with Albert, my life brought me to Dylan again. My first record-album assignment was *Music From Big Pink*, which had a painting by Dylan on the cover. I knew that everyone would read the credits to see his name and would then read my name next to his. That was when I realized that I was going to be well known. I was surprised.

Curiously, because our names are anagrams of each other—DYLAN/LANDY—many people thought I didn't exist— that he was me under an alias! There have even been articles about it.

Everyone liked the *Big Pink* photographs, and shortly afterward Al Aronowitz, a writer

AT HIS BYRDCLIFFE HOME

and friend of Dylan's, asked me to photograph Bob for the cover of *the Saturday Evening Post.*

I rented a little VW bug and drove up from the city to Bob's house in Woodstock. This was during the height of his fame, when he had been seen publicly only once in a couple of years, and many people thought he had died in a motorcycle accident.

Aronowitz introduced us. Bob told me how much he liked the Band photos, grabbed his guitar, sat on an old tire, and began playing while I took pictures. It occurred to me that millions of people would be thrilled to be ten feet away from Bob Dylan while he was playing, but he was so casual, it seemed normal to me. He suggested some other things. "This is what I do up here, take a picture," he said while putting the garbage cans away. He sat on the step of his equipment van and then in front of an old British cab he had. After a while he asked to use the camera. For some of the pictures I used infrared color film, which made the leaves bright red.

Although he was comfortable with me, he was nervous in front of the camera, and his uneasiness made it difficult for me. I was never the kind of photographer to talk people into feeling good, I let them be the way they were and photographed it. Usually it worked out, because I flowed with whatever mood they were in, without resistance until things lightened up.

He asked me to come back with the pictures when they were ready, which I did the following week. He liked the photos, and we started to hang out a bit. He suggested that I take photographs of him with Sara and the children. I don't think he had ever asked anyone else to do that. It seemed natural to me, and I was thrilled to photograph them because I thought they were a beautiful family. The value of the photos never entered my mind. I was immersed in the wonderful energy they had and felt joyous to document it. For many years afterward I resisted selling them, even though I was often in dire financial straits when I lived in Europe.

He was very happy, in love with his lovely and gracious wife, Sara, and with his family. He was hiding from the world, savoring the magical experience of having young children. That's why I didn't publish the pictures for many years. He cherished his privacy and didn't want any media attention on his family.

I was very impressed with Bob. He *was* a very special person. He intuitively understood what was going on in a situation. There was a feeling you got when you were with him that was exciting. I believe it was the flow of creative energy surrounding him that sort of spilled over onto you. Over the years I've seen him walk into rooms, even in the presence of other very famous people, and suddenly everyone's attention becomes totally focused on him. It's difficult to have this type of charisma: people always want a piece of you.

I remember admiring the way he dealt with his five-year-old son, Jesse, who was whining in frustration wanting Bob to help him move a toy car. I

SHOOTING THE PHOTOGRAPHER, W. JESSE

would have gone over and done it for him, but Bob encouraged him, "C'mon, Jesse, you can do it, just keep trying." And Jesse, with a big smile of satisfaction, did it. I was very impressed by Bob's instinct to teach him self-reliance.

We got pretty friendly, and I stayed overnight in his home three or four times. We talked about different things. When I asked him about politics, he told me he wasn't very interested in politics and didn't know much about it. I was shocked because his music was considered to be the Magna Carta of radical Sixties political thought. I asked him how he wrote those songs if he didn't know anything, and he said that he didn't create those ideas but simply "picked up what was in the air, and gave it back to people in another form." My interpretation is that he intuit-

ed the future of political thought and turned it into music—kind of like a seer singing poetry. His skill, he acknowledged, was "knowing how to use the language." Although he disclaimed having any interest in the political process, I felt he *was* interested in social justice.

About a year later, during another conversation at his house, he expressed some fairly conservative political views, which *really* surprised me. I couldn't believe it, but he seemed serious. However, while driving home, I ran into Richard Manuel of The Band, by chance. I told Richard what Bob had just said. Richard chuckled and told me Bob could have been putting me on, that he liked to put people on just to confuse them. I had observed that Bob liked to be mysterious because he felt it encouraged people to think for themselves. One of Bob's big themes in life was that people shouldn't blindly follow or accept things. So I never repeated what Bob told me, but I still wonder.

Another aspect of Dylan which impressed me was that he listened more than he talked. He brought someone out rather than talking about what he already knew. From seeing him do this, I understood that silence could be wiser than words.

I think this time in Woodstock was a transformative period for him. He was learning to feel and express love through his family experience. His music from this period reflects that: It's light, homey and havenlike. He was no longer heavy-handed. Woodstock is a very special place; the feeling in the air is wonderful. It has a history of spirituality going back to the Native Americans. The Tibetan Buddhists have established a center there because they feel it is on one of the main energy meridians in North America.

Just after the *Saturday Evening Post* shoot I moved to Woodstock. I had fallen in love with the lifestyle there and expected that I would do more work with Dylan and the Band. I used to see Bob occasionally here and there. One night I bumped into him and Sara as they were driving up to the Grand Union. He asked if I would mind going in and getting a few cans of cat food; they had just run out.

In early 1969 he called and asked me to take a picture for the back of his new album, *Nashville Skyline.* He had the front cover already picked out—a picture of the skyline of Nashville, where he had recorded the album.

We didn't know what to do; we had no concepts when we started. We met, and he suggested that we take a picture in front of the bakery in Woodstock with his son, Jesse, and two local Woodstock people. The brown leather jacket he was wearing was the same one he had worn for the covers of *John Wesley Harding* and *Blonde on Blonde.*

He was still uncomfortable being photographed, and therefore I was uncomfortable photographing him, but we stayed with it. We took some pictures at the bakery and then went to my house and hung out.

I projected some slides I had just taken of a female model, and he started to laugh. I asked him what was funny, and he said, "Don't you see the story?" "What story?" "Run them again."

As the pictures appeared, he wrote some captions and read them to me. They parlayed the

ELLIOTT LANDY BY BOB DYLAN

expressions on the woman's face into an absurdly funny dialogue. He wrote quickly for a while, throwing some pages away, perfecting the story,.which we both thought was incredibly funny. He said we should publish them.

After he left a little while later, he came right back and retrieved his discarded notes from the wastebasket. I wouldn't have thought to keep them, but I'm sure he had had some bad experiences.

I mentioned the project to him several times after that, but he said he couldn't find the notes. Over the years the photographs have disappeared as well.

That same day we took some photographs outside my house. He had his glasses on, but there wasn't any discussion about "I don't want to have the glasses on the album" or anything like that. We were just easy. It was very casual. He wanted some pictures, we took them, and neither of us conceptualized it. I'm spontaneous when I work, and so is he. An art director might have said, "Take the glasses off," but neither he nor I thought about it. However people present themselves is how I photograph them—I don't judge it.

Then on another afternoon I went over to his place. As we left the house, he grabbed a hat, and asked, "Do you think we could use this?" I had no idea if it would be good or not, so I told him "take it, and we'll see." We walked around through the woods behind his house looking for a good spot. It had just been raining, we had boots on, and he was carrying this hat.

He paused for a moment, apparently inspired, and said, "What about taking one from down there?" pointing to the ground. As I started kneeling, I saw that it was muddy but kept going. "Do you think I should wear this?" he asked, starting to put on his hat, smiling because it was kind of a goof, and he was having fun visualizing himself in this silly-looking traditional hat. "I don't know," I said as I snapped the shutter. It all happened so fast. If I had had any resistance in me, I would have missed the photograph that became the front cover. It is best to be open to life.

During those days in Woodstock he was really open and in a good mood. It was sunny out and we just followed our instincts. It was the first picture of him smiling, and in my opinion reflects the inner spirit, the loving essence of the man behind all the inspiring music he has given us. Someone told me that the reason people like it so much is that it makes them happy.

Every review of the album mentioned his smile on the cover. No one talked about the photograph itself. For me that is requisite for a "good" photograph. The medium itself should be invisible. It shouldn't make you look at it and think, "What a great photograph this is," but rather should make you focus on what is in the photograph: "Look at that child, look at the flower, look at that person, how fantastic."

Nearly everyone of my generation knows the photograph, and many have acknowledged it as an image that has had great meaning to them. Perhaps it reflects the love we were all seeking to find through making the world a better place.

And so this was a magical picture for all of us. It certainly assured my reputation as a photographer. My bill for the shoot, which in addition to

W. Anna, 1970

my fee, included an array of items such as gas, tolls, film, etc., came to exactly $777. In metaphysics 777 is the number of mystical manifestation, the magical number, representing mysteries, the occult, clairvoyance, magic, the seven principles of man, the universe, and also the notes on a musical scale. I was awed by this incredible coincidence. It strengthened my feeling that everything is interconnected in ways which the logical mind cannot explain: We are all one.

I brought the picture to CBS Records and told them that Dylan didn't want any writing on the cover, no names, logos, or other sales tools. This was Bob's way of saying that his music was not created as a commercial pursuit. Despite his wishes, CBS put their logo in the upper left-hand corner, and although small and seemingly insignificant, this ruins the three-dimensionality of the image. While looking at the record, cover the logo, then uncover and cover it again. It will appear to go from two to three dimensions and back.

The following summer, in 1970, he called and asked me if I would photograph some of his drawings. He had started painting in Woodstock some years before. I thought his work was very beautiful. His drawings reminded me of Van Gogh's. Looking back at it now, I find this similarity interesting, as Van Gogh was obsessive about the purity and spirituality of his painting, while Dylan is the same about the purity of his music, treating it with reverence, to be given in pure form to the people, not adulterated by commercial interests. This is why he has never sold any of his songs for commercials, one of the few artists to maintain that purity of pur-

82

pose which the planet needs to survive.

A few weeks later Al Aronowitz called from Bob's and asked me to come over to help set up a trampoline. Bob had moved into a newer, brighter, and more spacious house. We set up the trampoline, and Bob asked me to take some pictures of the kids and then some of him doing some funny stuff. It was a great day.

In the fall both he and I moved to Manhattan. One time he came over to my loft, hidden under a knit cap and dark glasses. It was a different Dylan than I had known in Woodstock. He invited us (my wife and year-old daughter) to a birthday party at his MacDougal Street home. We went, had a fun day, and said we'd see each other again soon, but shortly after that he went to Mexico to make a film, and I left for Europe, where I stayed for seven years.

In 1978, when I returned from Europe, I went to a concert, but wasn't allowed to see him. After the concert, by chance, I met him in the elevator backstage as he was going to a party. He said hello, but didn't invite me along when he got out. Since then we've spoken occasionally, but our connection has never been renewed, and I'm sorry for the lost opportunity to do creative work. Bob was always suggesting that we do pictures and words together, but somehow the projects never happened.

BYRDCLIFF HOME, 1968

W. JESSE AND MARIA

w. Sara & Jesse 1968

w. Jesse, 1968

OUTSIDE MY HOUSE, WOODSTOCK, 1969

W. FRIENDS & JESSE, WOODSTOCK BAKERY, 1969

w. Anna, 1970

ON THE TRAMPOLINE, OHAYO MTN. RD. HOME, WOODSTOCK, 1970

W. SAM AND ANNA, 1970

"TAKE ONE OF
ME LIKE THIS."
1970

BYRDCLIFF, SATURDAY EVENING POST COVER PHOTO, 1968

BOB DYLAN,1968, INFRARED FILM

GARTH HUDSON

ROBBIE ROBERTSON

RICK DANKO

RICHARD MANUEL

RICHARD MANUEL

THE BAND, FILLMORE EAST, 1969

JOHN LEE HOOKER, NYC, 1969, INFRARED FILM

ALBERT AYLER, BKLYN, NYC, 1969, INFRARED FILM

Van & Janet Morrison w. Peter

Van Morrison, Moondance album photo

JANIS JOPLIN W. BIG BROTHER & THE HOLDING CO., FILLMORE EAST, NYC, 1968

PROCOL HAREM, ANDERSON THEATER, NYC, 1968

JANIS JOPLIN, ANDERSON THEATER, 1968

ALL WITH
JOSHUA LIGHT SHOW

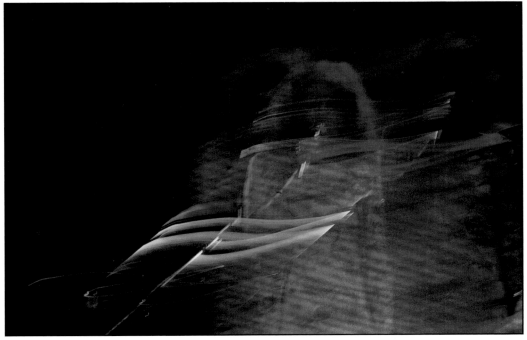

GRACE SLICK, FILLMORE EAST, 1968

Woodstock
An Aquarian Exposition

Early in August 1969, Mike Lang rode his motorcycle over to my house in Woodstock and asked if I would be interested in photographing a festival he was planning. It was one of the most important yeses I ever said. We didn't talk about money except to say that we would work it out. It wasn't even a handshake—it was preordained.

3 Days of Peace & Music

August 15, 16, 17, 1969 – Bethel, New York

On August 15, 16, and 17, 1969, nearly 500,000 people gathered together to celebrate life. They came looking for music and new ways. They found a hard path—there were miles to walk; rain and mud; not much food to eat, nor shelter to sleep beneath; life was not as they usually knew it.

But something happened. There was peace and harmony despite conditions that might have set off riots. Most everyone lived in consideration and enjoyment with everyone else. Woodstock became a symbol to the world of a better way of life—of freedom, of love, of spiritual union between many. There was hope.

Years have passed. "What has happened...where has Woodstock gone?" Words are heard: "It was a fluke." "It can never happen again." "It was not real."

The coming of a new consciousness is a slow process. Woodstock is a way of thinking, a way of being—kindness, consideration, sharing and enjoying; life as it should be and would be if we lived that way.

Astrologically, the birth of the age of Aquarius is upon us—an age of peace and understanding, a golden age. Like all births, the birth of this new consciousness is difficult. Old ways are falling as new ways evolve. The time of labor nears. A soft seedling must break

through a hard seed shell. A baby comes through a birth which can be painful.

Change is often difficult, but what is outside the new door is usually better than what was behind the old. We are given habits by the culture we grow in, the physical realities of our planet, and the needs we have. With the coming of new, clean technologies, physical wants can be met — people no longer have to fight to survive. There can be enough for everyone.

Woodstock showed us that people can live together in a peaceful and sharing way. It showed that the goal many were going toward during those years was reachable. It actually happened for 500,000 peo-

ple at one time for three days.

The mystical teachings tell us that with the birth of each age there is a sign, a teacher, which appears to lead the way. As Christ was the example for a world 2,000 years ago, so the experience at Woodstock can be an example for our world today. Just as the birth of Jesus could find no place, so, too, Woodstock was without welcome—yet both found their destined place to be—one in Bethlehem, the other in Bethel; the similarity of names whispering to us of a cosmic declaration, an intelligence beyond our own, telling us that our ideals could be made real, that a new time was approaching— telling us to keep on trying.

WOODSTOCK

BEFORE THE RAIN

CLIMBING THE SOUND TOWERS

DAVID
CLAYTON-
THOMAS,
BLOOD,
SWEAT &
TEARS

TEN YEARS AFTER

JANIS JOPLIN, PERFORMER'S PAVILION

JIMI
HENDRIX,
FILLMORE
EAST, 196

MAX YASGUR, OWNER OF WOODSTOCK FESTIVAL SITE, AND MARTIN SCORSESE (RETURNING PEACE SIGN)

JOE
COCKER

CLIMBING THE SOUND TOWER

AUDIENCE MEMBER RUSHES THE STAGE

MIKE LANG (CENTER), CREATOR OF THE FESTIVAL

CANNED HEAT

JOAN BAEZ, PREGNANT, WOODSTOCK

JANIS
JOPLIN AT
WOODSTOCK

RAVI SHANKAR

BRIDGE TO THE PERFORMERS' PAVILION

JOHNNY WINTER

IN THE RAIN, RAVI SHANKAR

MELANIE

LEVON
HELM
& THE
BAND

GARTH HUDSON

ARLO GUTHRIE

Moving On

While working with The Band and Dylan, I spent a lot of time in the town of Woodstock in upstate New York, fell in love with it, and decided to move there. I found a lovely house at the end of a dead-end road, exactly what I had been looking for.

Life was sweet. The spirituality of the place took me over and transformed my life. I grew tired of taking photographs of musicians and being involved with the music industry. I yearned to return to my original inspiration for taking photographs–to show beauty to people.

As a way of escaping from the commercial demands of photography, I opened a small gallery in Woodstock, with the intention of showing my photographs and paintings. During that period I discovered the world of metaphysics and spirituality. I found that many of the ancient wisdoms and Oriental health practices had validity for my life. I became totally fascinated with books such as the *I Ching*, the Edgar Cayce readings, *Be Here Now, The Aquarian Gospel of Jesus The Christ, The Urantia Book*, the *Tao Te Ching, Talks by Krishnamurti*, books on astrology, the tarot, the kabala, natural health care, macrobiotics, yoga, tai chi, etc. I felt that people should know about these things, and the gallery turned into a metaphysical bookshop as I followed my passion.

I was happy to sit in the bookshop and talk with people who came by but whenever I was recognized as "Elliott Landy, the photographer," I quickly changed the conversation. I wanted to be related to for who I was, not for my connection to famous people, and I wasn't interested in exhibiting or talking about my music photographs. In order to move on to another period of my life and art, I had to free my mind and dissociate myself from my previous success.

I wanted to photograph what I found beautiful in the normal course of my own life, not what was shown to me through media. I was through photographing someone else's art form or someone else's war. This period of totally personal photography began with pictures of my newly born daughter and continued for seven years on the road in Europe, where we lived and traveled in a forty-passenger bus. During this time I was inspired by the beauty of my children and wanted to share it with others. I tried to make people aware of the importance of children and family life through my photographs of innocence and love.

After the children began to grow up, my photography became more experimental and abstract, although I occasionally did jobs in the music business when someone found me.

Today in addition to photographing an occasional musician who inspires or pays me, I continue to work with children, multiple imagery, motion, and kaleidoscopic lenses to create images which reflect purity, innocence, and non-attachment to perceived normal reality. I feel it is important, that people have a vision of life which allows more hope and more opportunity than are available in the images presented by newspapers and television.

In 1970 I discovered a style of combining moving images with music so that the motion of the images was syncopated with the rhythms of the music. This visual music work forms the basis of an interactive music-visual system I am developing today.

Life is good, I'm living in Woodstock again with a wonderful lady in a beautiful home with a view of the mountains, caretaking my vintage work. But sometimes I find myself wishing I could find something that would involve me as totally as still photography did in years past. At 50 I still feel young, but I don't have the need to *do* art anymore. If I want to, that's fine, but I don't *need* to, like I did.

Recently I saw my old photo-credit stamp on the back of a print, and it brought that feeling of total immersion back to me: I lived in two and a half rooms at 88th St. and Broadway in New York City, in a street-level apartment with soot-covered windows and car noise outside.

I lived there until I met Bob Dylan and The Band and decided to move to Woodstock. By that time I had taken many of the photos which today are history to a new generation.

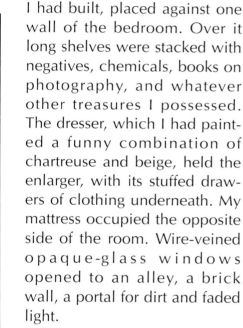

In those days there was nothing else. Shoot, go home to process the film, go out and shoot some more, give the prints to the newspaper, and do more. I loved doing pictures and having them published right away in the newspapers I was working with. No hassle, no wait, no pay. But what joy. To do work and see it in a place where others could see it too.

Eventually the business of rock 'n' roll photography turned me off. I gave my heart, and the people who wrote the checks never appreciated it, and people who had no vision usually controlled the artwork. Perhaps I'll find some way to get back to it someday—to do work and show it to people in a pure way, not one dictated by someone's imagined commercial needs.

My success with The Band and Dylan came because Albert Grossman used his leverage to take control of the album-cover process. Only the artistic inspiration which bounced back and forth between the musicians and myself determined which pictures would be used. It was fun.

These are pictures of what was, of people like myself who were doing things because they loved to do them. It was "groovy," as we used to say, doing what we loved, but also we had no choice—we had to, our inner needs were too strong. And they still are.

So when I saw the photo-credit stamp with my old address on it, I realized that most of my famous photographs were taken while I was living in a near dungeon of a place, but to me it felt like heaven. My darkroom was an eight-foot sink I had built, placed against one wall of the bedroom. Over it long shelves were stacked with negatives, chemicals, books on photography, and whatever other treasures I possessed. The dresser, which I had painted a funny combination of chartreuse and beige, held the enlarger, with its stuffed drawers of clothing underneath. My mattress occupied the opposite side of the room. Wire-veined opaque-glass windows opened to an alley, a brick wall, a portal for dirt and faded light.

But in that room, in that atmosphere, I was ecstatic, printing from late nights till early mornings, listening to Bob Fass on WBAI playing "Light My Fire," and occasionally calling him up with news from the underground. How can I describe it? Innocence, belief, faith? I felt I was part of something that was changing the world. I was right, and I was wrong—it didn't happen as fast as I thought it would, but it is *still* happening.

The Essence of Woodstock
—by Richie Havens

Woodstock started out as a normal festival. Most of us who had been booked to play there expected it to be just another festival, the kind popularized in the movie *Monterey Pop*, which had just been released.

The guy who drove us up to the site had hired twenty cars besides his own. We left very early that morning—around 5:30—and I was glad we did. I never would have made it there otherwise. There were two motels across the highway from each other, about seven miles away from the field, and we musicians stayed there and waited for the cars to come and take our equipment and gear to the field.

But when it came time for us to play, the road to get to the field was totally blocked by cars and people walking to the concert site, and there was no way to get the singers or the equipment to the stage.

We were already about an hour late when the first helicopter came down right outside my hotel window at the Howard Johnson's, and I was told that since I had the fewest instruments, I should go over first. It was a private helicopter. They had gotten some guy down the road who had a bubble helicopter, a big glass bubble, and he took us over. We packed into this bubble— two conga drums, two guitars, and three musicians, plus the pilot—and we just took off and headed for the field.

We flew over all of those people, and when I looked down at all the different colors, it looked like the world's largest Leroy Niemann painting. I said, "You know, this time they're not gonna be able to hide us. They're not gonna be able to make it look like a little thing." We had

numbers this time. I could see that from the air. This time we were going to make the news in a positive way.

We landed backstage. I was supposed to be fifth on the bill, but Michael Lang knew he had to get somebody onstage, since the bands with the big equipment couldn't get through, so I was the candidate.

He chased me around, and I finally consented to help him out and to go on first. But I told him, "The first beer can that comes up on stage, Michael, you're gonna owe me, 'cuz your concert is late, and they're gonna get me for it. Right?"

But fortunately people were so happy that something was gonna happen, that somebody was finally gonna play music, that they really were warm and welcoming to me as a musician. I had already made two albums, so I was fairly well known at that point. I went on stage and I started singing.

Two hours and forty minutes later, as I went off for the eighth time, they said, "No, go back, nobody else is here yet!" So I went back out for the eighth time, but I really didn't know what I was gonna sing. So I sat down on the stool, I strummed my guitar a little bit, I tuned up, and what happened was that I looked out over the crowd, and I saw the freedom that we thought we wanted to obtain being displayed right in front of me. We already had the freedom. And that was the essence of my experience, realizing that we were exercising this freedom that we had been trying to get since the early Sixties. So that's what I sang: "Freedom, freedom," just letting the word flow out over the crowd like that, over and over again.

The essence of Woodstock was not sex, drugs, and rock and roll. That was the press's take on what happened there. The essence of Woodstock was bringing people of like mind together, into a place where they were gonna enjoy music, most of which they didn't even know and had never even heard before. But it wasn't just the music that brought them there. Woodstock was in essence a coming together, a gathering, a giant be-in. It was a people's festival, I would call it the first American people's festival, where the people came together to celebrate their essences, their concerns, and their feelings for the world around them.

So to me Woodstock had a very deep meaning. No one had ever seen 400,000 people get together in one field without having a riot. The essence of Woodstock was that we accomplished what we had started out to do in the early Sixties, which was to show that we, as young people, were not going to back down from our political feelings, our emotional feelings, and our newly discovered citizenry.

Rock 'n' roll was the first generational primal scream. Woodstock was an envelope of consciousness, a way of being. We had a different view of the world and we wanted people to know that the world wasn't as negative as most people thought—that there were a lot of positive things that we could make happen for the betterment of our planet and the world around us.

The world wasn't gonna change overnight. We never expected it to. To bring about the kind of changes we were looking for immediately, a flying saucer would have to land to scare us all into being one world. But I do think that the spirit of Woodstock has saturated the world just about, and has served the purpose of awakening minds to the fact that they, too, have the right to celebrate, they, too, have the right to have their own Woodstocks.

As far as I'm concerned, everyone now is a product of the Woodstock spirit, and there is no way they can get around it. Our doctors have been to Woodstock, our nurses have been to Woodstock, our lawyers have been to Woodstock. Even our judges and police—or at least some of them—have been to Woodstock. And little by little, that spirit — that sense of calm spirituality that came out of Woodstock and permeated our personalities—is very much alive and very much a part of our every day, our every moment.

RICHIE HAVENS, AUGUST 15, 1969, BETHEL, NY

MY GRATITUDE TO:

Lisette Modell, my first photography teacher, whose appreciation for my early photographs gave me the confidence to do more.
Larence Shustak, for teaching me the art of photography and the attitude of life.
Peter Moore, photographer, whose humble manner taught me much.
Leslie Landy, who helped me escape to a better place in life.
All my friends and co-conspirators from the sixties.
Jim Ferretti, for being the generous master of so many things.
Andras Nevai, for being the healer that he is.
Annette Maxberry, for always being there for me and many others.
Werner Mark Linz of Continuum for his publishing wisdom.
Rob Baker of Continuum for his editorial guidance.
Alice Linz, who had the vision to mention me to her father.
Annie Berthold-Bond & Green Alternatives Magazine, for their efforts to help heal the planet.
Kelly Sinclair, for helping me organize and evaluate my work.
Daia Gerson, for her clear copy editing
Wolf Baschung & **Ben Caswell:** B/W prints.
Color by **Clone-a-Chrome, Time-Life Labs.**
Elliott Landy is represented by **Laura Zimzores**

Jonathon Bachrach, Bob Bettendorf, Suzan Cooper, Dalton Delan, Bo Hahn, Niko Hansen, Klaus Humann, Diana & Peter Insalaco, Virginia Lohle, Pat Lucas, Diane Maier, Grazia Neri, Yael Oestreich, Orion Press, Redferns, Emerson Sparks, Upstate Films, and to my Woodstock neighbors, who make each day pleasant....